Children on the Front Lines of Justice

Report Sexual Abuse and Survive the Criminal Trial

Eliza Sultan, Author

Kelly Jensen, Editor

Children on the Front Line of Justice:

Report Sexual Abuse and Survive the Criminal Trial

Second Edition ISBN 9781666411379

Copyright © 2024 by Eliza Sultan

All rights reserved. No part of this publication may be reproduced in part or in whole or transmitted in any form or by any means, electronic or mechanical, including photocopying, recording, or via any information storage retrieval system now known or to be invented, without permission in writing from the author, except by a reviewer who wishes to quote brief passages in connection with a review written for inclusion in a print or online magazine, newspaper, or broadcast.

For press inquiries or other information, please contact elizaasultan@gmail.com

Printed in the United States of America

Editor: Kelly Jensen
Book designer: Mark D'Antoni
Illustrator: Kilson Spany

While the stories portrayed in this book are true, some of the names (people, companies, schools, locations) and identifying details have been changed to protect confidentiality.

STATE OF NEW MEXICO
OFFICE OF THE ATTORNEY GENERAL

HECTOR H. BALDERAS
ATTORNEY GENERAL

November 17, 2022

As New Mexico's Attorney General, I have prioritized prosecuting criminals who commit violent crime, and particularly those who harm children. While one aspect of this work is naturally holding bad actors accountable, my main focus has been giving a voice and support to survivors and victims of the worst crimes. When my office brings a case, we truly want to shed light on the impact of what has happened to the family and community members involved. When Eliza Sultan, the author of this book, bravely came and shared her family's story with me, I knew that we needed to take immediate action and do everything in our power to bring justice and use our authority to make her family's story heard.

I've had the privilege of working with many families, but when I spoke with Eliza I knew that her family was especially strong. I cannot adequately convey in words the bravery of her and her children in seeking justice for the incredible pain and suffering they experienced, but I knew that their strength would extend beyond their case and that they had the power to support families just like theirs. Their advocacy, for themselves and for others, has inspired me to continue to work with her on systemic policy change that will open the eyes of policymakers and community members to the horrible realities families face when seeking justice. We will continue to work to change New Mexico law, making court processes that address the realities of the trauma that children face when having to testify against a loved one who has hurt them.

I am confident that we have supported Eliza and given her family a voice, and I am proud that this book will serve as a powerful tool that elevates the difficult experiences of children who are forced to testify in a court case. This story shows the humanity of a family going through this process, and there is no doubt in my mind that others who need support will be inspired with hope by the courage shown by this honorable family.

Respectfully,

Hector Balderas

Foreword

When Eliza asked me to write a foreword to this book, I was honored, humbled and a bit intimidated. I have spent much of my 25-year career specializing in prosecuting the offenders of the most despicable crimes against children. Despite my years of experience, I have never felt that I was able to completely bring justice and healing to these small victims. Although I have been instrumental in sending many offenders to prison, thereby bringing some small amount of closure to the victims and their families, I have always been keenly aware that the damage done, and harm caused to these kids cause wounds and leave deep, long-lasting scars that the criminal justice system is not equipped to mend. In fact, the judicial system often re-victimizes those it is supposed to protect. In many states, such as New Mexico, children are required to testify in open court in front of their abuser. My inspiration has always come from these brave young children who have pushed their fears aside to testify about things that no child should even know about. I applaud Eliza for her steadfast support of her kids. Unfortunately, not all abused children are supported by the non-offending adults in their lives. It is well established that the kids who are supported are most likely to make a full recovery from their trauma. The first-person narrative of this book tells a story that is all too familiar to professionals who deal with these cases. Yet, despite the familiarity of the tale, it is important to recognize that each child's experience and pain is uniquely his/her own and so must be their healing. The most important thing we can do to start that healing is to believe them and protect them when they speak out. In an ideal world, this book would not be needed. In an ideal world every child would be safe from the harm caused by those who steal their childhood. Until the day that world exists, we must do more than teach our children to speak up—we must believe them and support them in their journey to healing.

Barbara Romo
District Attorney, 13th Judicial District
Cibola, Sandoval & Valencia Counties, New Mexico

My name is May. This is a story about something that happened to my big brother Charlie and me when we were four and seven years old.

I love Christmas. The holiday lights are majestic.

I had been asking Mama to go down to the Plaza to look at the Christmas lights with our Poppy, my big brother Charlie, and me together like a family.

My parents are divorced. Sometimes, Mama would agree to go on a family outing.

I feel sad that my parents are divorced. Sometimes I just wish I had a normal family where my parents got along with each other.

Before Poppy moved out, the four of us lived in the apartment together. Now that they got divorced, Mama, Charlie and I live in public housing near downtown.

I remember them fighting a lot before he moved out.

Poppy was mean when he got mad. He would throw plates, sometimes hit Mama, and yell when he got angry. I felt sad and scared to see my parents fighting.

When our Poppy moved out, Charlie and I would go to his house on the weekends. At first it was fun. He would play a lot

of games and tickle us. He always gave us candy and other sweet treats.

Then one day he told us that some of the games we played together had to be a secret. He gave us candy if we promised to keep these games a secret. The types of games we played made me feel icky. I didn't like the way he touched my private parts. He made us promise we'd keep this as a special secret just between the three of us.

One day I overheard Mama talking on the phone to her brother, our Uncle Hank. After she hung up the phone, she called Charlie and me into the living room. She asked us to sit down on the couch next to her. Charlie asked if we were in trouble. "Of course not," Mama said. "I want to talk to you about why Uncle Hank just called. Since he owns martial arts schools, sometimes he takes classes to learn new ways to teach kids. He just finished a class about how to talk to kids about what's safe for their bodies. Uncle Hank wanted me to share with you what learned. He's my big brother, so he still tells me what to do."

Mama told us that our bodies are sacred and belong only to us. She said that nobody could touch our bodies without our permission. She told us that if anyone ever touched these private parts without our permission that it was called **child sexual abuse**. She said it was against the law to hurt a child. She explained that if anyone touched either of our butts, my vagina or Charlie's penis that we needed to tell a **safe adult.**

That afternoon we sat around the kitchen table together and drank chamomile tea and ate gingersnaps cookies. We made a list together of the safe adults we could tell if anyone ever touched us on those private body parts. We listed Grandma, the teachers at pre-school, Pastor Harry, or Mama.

After Mama talked to us about body safety, I started thinking about the way Poppy touched us.

I liked the games that Poppy played with us, especially the candy he gave us, but now I knew deep down that he was doing something wrong by touching our private parts.

I felt sad. I felt scared. I felt confused.

Poppy always reminded us that we had to keep these games a secret. He even threatened to hurt Mama, Charlie, and me if we told anybody.

But I love my Poppy and didn't want him to get into trouble.

Charlie and I started counting down to his fifth birthday. He was excited for his party and for his piñata.

Child Sexual Abuse: when a perpetrator intentionally harms a minor physically, psychologically, sexually, or by acts of neglect, the crime is known as child abuse.

Safe Adult: someone a child can go to if they ever feel unsafe, have ever been hurt, or if they're not sure if a situation is unsafe.

Charlie's birthday party was in the community room in our apartment complex. Some of the neighborhood kids and their families came. We sat outside under the shaded awning. We played games and ate cake. We all took turns hitting the piñata with a broomstick. The candy flew in every direction, and everyone scrambled to grab a handful.

After the party, Charlie asked Mama if he could go for the night to Poppy's house alone. Mama was surprised by his

request but said it was okay. She called Poppy and told him to come by the house to get Charlie. Charlie seemed nervous. Poppy showed up with balloons and presents. He gave a pink balloon to me, and that made me happy.

I got to spend time alone with Mama. That was special. We colored and ate mac n' cheese.

It was strange that Charlie asked to go to Poppy's alone. I now understand that he was probably trying to protect me.

I'd been trying to get the words out to tell someone that my Poppy was touching my private parts. I had told two of my pre-school teachers that Poppy was touching my bichu and my bunda, but they didn't understand what I was telling them. Bichu and bunda are the Portuguese words our Poppy taught us for our private parts. Bichu is a slang word for vagina, and bunda is a word for butt.

I was laying on the bed after Mama gave me a bath. Mama was putting corn starch on my body. I blurted out "Poppy touches my bichu and it hurts."

Mama looked very surprised. She didn't ask me a lot of questions. She hugged me and told me she was proud of me for telling her. She told me she would protect Charlie and me. I felt scared. I felt relieved. I had finally told someone.

I could overhear Mama making a call from the other bedroom. When she came out, she said, "May, don't be scared. I just talked to your counselor about what you told me. She said that I have to call the police to tell them."

I could tell Mama was scared, but she did what my counselor told her to do. She believed me. She told the police.

Later that evening, a tall policeman in uniform came to our apartment. Mama put me in bed with a movie and told me to stay in the bedroom. I was worried about Charlie being alone with Poppy. I was worried that Poppy was going to be in trouble. I was scared that he would hurt us now that I had told on him.

After the policeman left, Mama came into the bedroom. She lay down next to me. She had tears on her face. She said,

"May, you're very brave for telling me. I'm proud of you. I'm going to keep you safe."

The next morning, I was so relieved when I saw Poppy's car pull-up in front of our apartment. Poppy stayed in the car. Charlie knocked on the door. Mama opened the door. Charlie was standing in the doorway. He had chocolate stains on his cheeks. He came into the house holding a balloon. I hugged him tight.

Mama sat down on the couch with both of us. She was very serious, and she spoke very quickly. She put her arms around us.

"Charlie, last night May told me something very serious. She told me that Poppy has been touching her vagina. This is called sexual abuse. I had to call the police."

Mama was in a hurry to get us ready. She was more stressed than usual. "Mama, where are we going?"

"We're going a place like the doctor's office. They're going to check you and Charlie to make sure you're okay."

We drove across town. Mama liked to listen to country

music in the car. Usually, we asked her to change the music. Today we listened. We were all quiet.

I had knots in my tummy. I knew this had to do with what I had told Mama about Poppy touching my private parts. My heart was racing. I felt terrified. I didn't know what was going to happen next.

We arrived at a big, gray building. There were flower planters and colorful sculptures in the yard. There was a jungle gym and swings behind a small, white fence.

There was a police car parked in front. The same policeman who'd come to our house last night got out of his police car. He stepped out of the car to greet us. I saw that he had two stuffed animals in his hands.

"Good morning, Ma'am. I have these stuffies for May and Charlie. Is that alright?"

Mama smiled and said "Yes. Thank you. That's so thoughtful of you."

"May, Charlie, this is Officer Santana. He's here to help us and to keep us safe."

We hid behind Mama and peeked from around her leg. Officer Santana knelt to our eye level. He extended the stuffed animals. He smiled. "You're very brave. We're going to do everything we can to protect you."

Mama reminded us to make eye contact and thank Officer Santana. She was always reminding us about manners.

We followed Officer Santana into the building. The waiting room was full of books, toys, and beanbag chairs.

There was a shelf with snacks. They looked like yummy snacks, the kind of snacks Mama didn't allow us to eat.

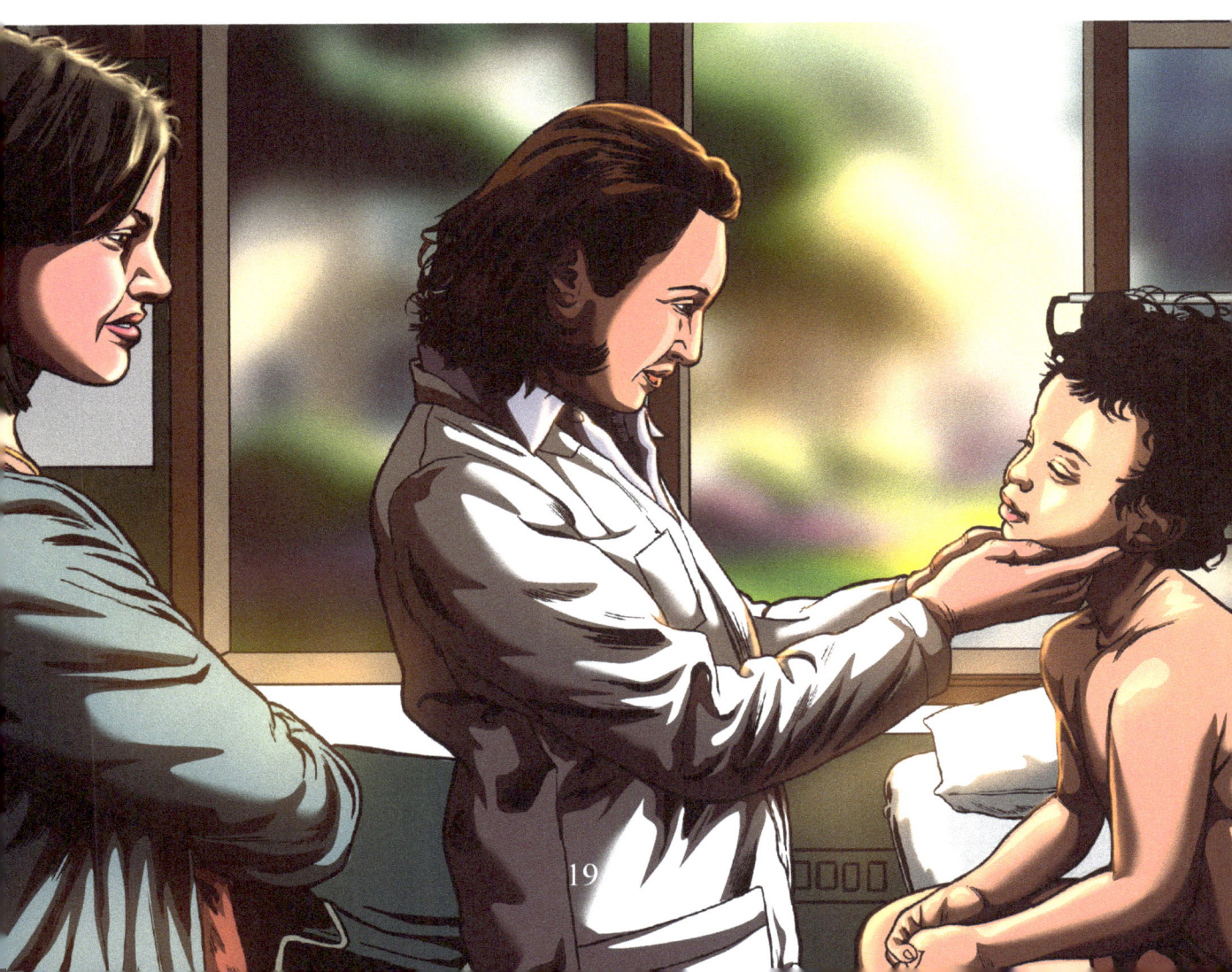

Parts of this day are blurry now. I remember meeting the nurse. She introduced herself to us. Her name was Jackie. She said she was a **sexual assault nurse examiner.** Nurse Jackie explained to us that she was going to examine our private

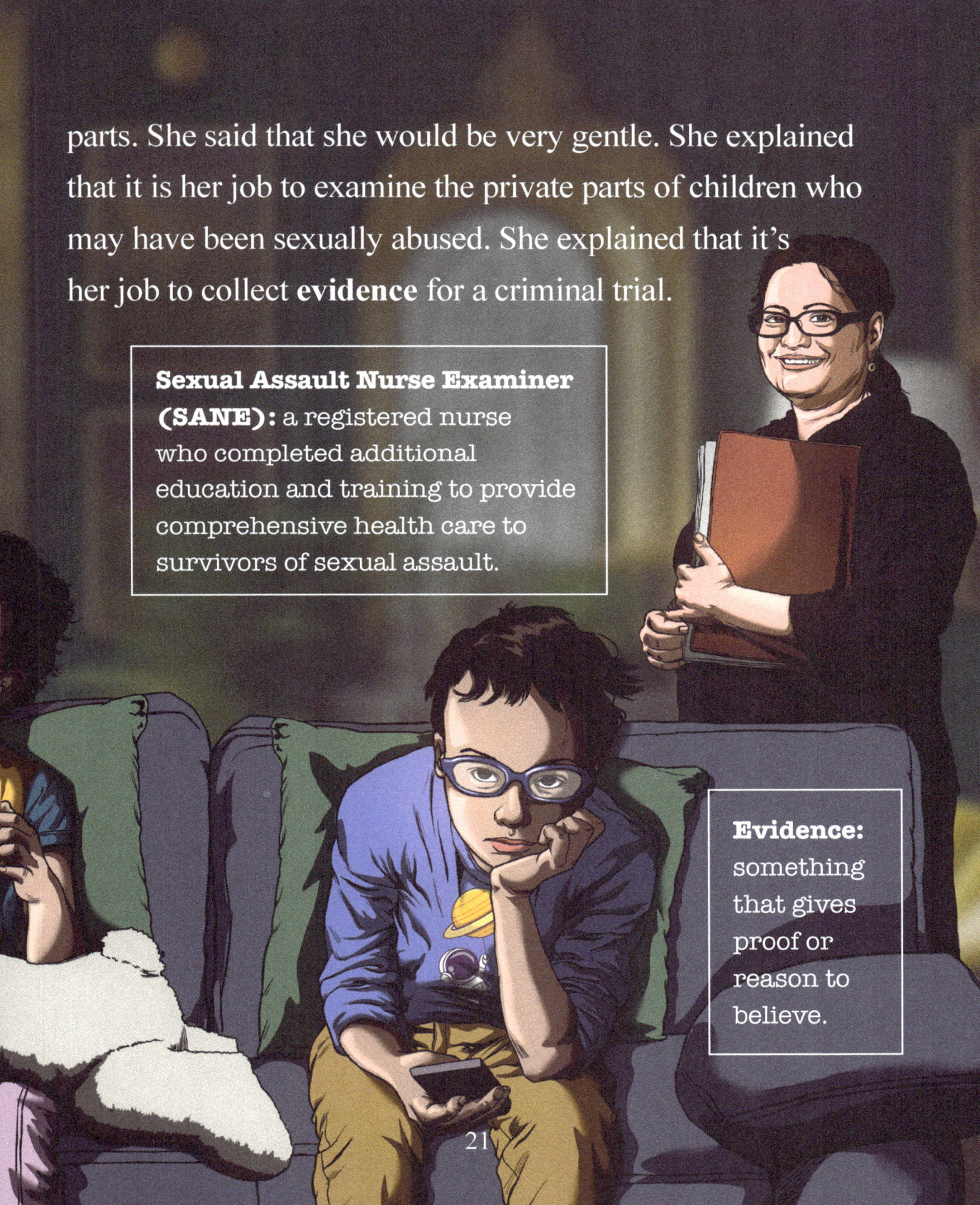

parts. She said that she would be very gentle. She explained that it is her job to examine the private parts of children who may have been sexually abused. She explained that it's her job to collect **evidence** for a criminal trial.

Sexual Assault Nurse Examiner (SANE): a registered nurse who completed additional education and training to provide comprehensive health care to survivors of sexual assault.

Evidence: something that gives proof or reason to believe.

Mama was allowed to sit in the room during the exam. We had to take off our clothes. Nurse Jackie gave us gowns, like the ones in the hospital. She examined both Charlie and me. She looked at our private parts with magnifying glasses and took photos. She was gentle, and it wasn't as scary as I thought it would be.

After the exam Nurse Jackie talked to Mama. She told her that she had found physical evidence of penetration or sexual abuse. She told Mama that our lives would be changed forever. She explained that Charlie and I would have to **testify** in front of our Poppy in court. I don't think Mama understood what most of this meant.

Testify: to make a solemn declaration or affirmation, esp. under oath.

After the exam, we took a break and went into the room with the beanbags and the yummy snacks. Mama allowed us to have something sweet. We read a book together, and then we went outside to play on the swing set.

Officer Santana came outside and asked us to come back inside. A **social worker** from **child protective services** talked to us. She explained that it is her job to make sure we were safe while the police were conducting their investigation. She told us we wouldn't be seeing our Poppy for a while. I felt sad and relieved.

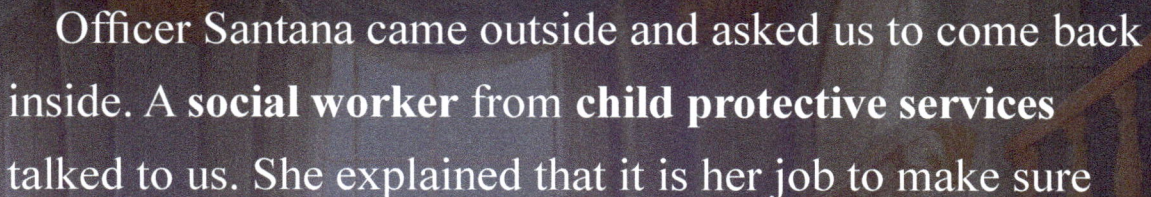

Social Worker: a worker who promotes the well-being of society, as by assisting the underprivileged or disadvantaged.

Child Protective Services: a branch of your state's social services department that is responsible for the assessment, investigation, and intervention regarding cases of child abuse and neglect, including sexual abuse.

> **Forensic Interviewer:** A forensic interview is a non-leading, developmentally sensitive method of gathering information from children. These recorded statements are conducted by a specially trained, unbiased professional in a legally defensible manner.

It was a long day. Next Charlie and I each met with a **forensic interviewer.** She was a nice lady, who said she had kids close to our ages. Mama wasn't allowed to come in. She said the interview was being recorded, and Officer Santana was sitting on the other side of the one-way glass that looked like a mirror. The forensic interviewer asked questions about what happened with Poppy. I felt squirmy. I didn't like talking about my Poppy touching me. The interview didn't last long. I just told her the icky stuff I remembered. I was happy to see Mama when the interview was over.

> **Prosecutor:** an attorney who prosecutes, esp. when serving as an official of a county, district, or other government entity.

One day after school, Mama told us that we were going to meet with the **prosecutor** in a place called Las Vegas. We had to go on a long car ride.

Mama explained that because Las Vegas was where Poppy lived, and where the sexual abuse took place, that's where the trial would take place.

Mama told us that there was a fun city called Las Vegas in Nevada, but the Las Vegas we were going to was in New Mexico.

In Las Vegas we met with the **deputy district attorney**, who would be prosecuting the case. The building had thick glass. It smelled stale. It seemed like everyone was serious.

We met with two women. One was named Ashley, who was a **victim advocate** and K.C., the Deputy District Attorney. I asked what all this meant. K.C. explained

Deputy District Attorney: an assistant who works under the supervision of a district attorney in carrying out prosecution duties for both misdemeanor and felony court cases.

> **Victim Advocate:** a person, whether paid or serving as a volunteer, who provides services to victims of domestic violence, sexual assault, stalking, or dating violence under the auspices or supervision of a victim services program.
>
> **Victims:** someone who is hurt, injured, or killed by a person, group, or event.
>
> **Perpetrate/d:** to commit or carry out (a crime, act of mischief, or the like).
>
> **Survivor:** a person who continues to function.
>
> **Traumatic:** an emotional shock that has a deep effect on one's life for a long time.
>
> **Resiliency:** the capacity to withstand and recover quickly from difficulty, sickness, or the like.
>
> **Justice:** the upholding of what is just, fair, and right.

that Charlie and I were **victims**. She explained that a victim is someone who had a crime **perpetrated** against them.

K.C. told us that someday we would be **survivors** instead of victims. Ashley explained that a survivor is someone who's been through something **traumatic**, like sexual abuse. She said that we wouldn't become survivors overnight. She used a lot of big words I didn't understand, like **resiliency**, being believed and getting **justice**. She said that someday we would be able to make peace with the things that happened between us and Poppy.

On some of our trips to Las Vegas we would meet with Ashley and K.C. in the park behind the District Attorney's Office. That wasn't as scary as the big room with the long conference table.

Mama would sit on one bench in the park. Charlie and I would sit with K.C. and Ashley on another bench. They'd ask us questions about the details of what we remembered Poppy doing to us. Talking about it made me feel squirmy. Even today it still sometimes bothers me if I think about it too much.

After those meetings we'd always go for ice cream. Charlie and I would ask Mama what we were supposed to say at the trial. Over and over, she said the same words. "I cannot tell you what to say. All I can tell you is to be brave. Tell the truth. Tell what you remember, and you will be okay."

When I felt nervous about testifying, Mama repeated herself.

"I cannot tell you what to say. All I can tell you is to be brave. Tell the truth. Tell what you remember, and you will be okay."

Courthouse: a building where courts of law and other government offices are located.

Metal Detector: a device that detects and signals the presence of metal objects and is used to discover concealed weapons at a security point.

Witness Stand: the place in a court of law from which a witness testifies.

Judge: a person trained to hear and decide cases brought before a court of law.

Preside (Over a) Trial: to act as the one in charge of the act of hearing a case in court to decide whether a person has broken a particular law.

While I wasn't sure that everything was okay, Mama tried her best to reassure us that we were okay and safe.

On a couple of our visits to Las Vegas, K.C. and Ashley took us to this big building called the **courthouse**. It was a towering stone building that made me feel small. There was a **metal detector** and big men with uniforms like police officers. They wore guns on their waistbands. We put our bags and jackets on the metal detector.

I asked one of the men why he wore a gun on his belt. He explained that it is his job to keep everyone safe in the courthouse. He said that sometimes people get very mad. He said he helps to keep the courthouse safe and orderly. I know about what mad looks like when it's unsafe because sometimes Poppy was scary when he got mad. I was glad the policemen were in the courthouse.

My brother and I were anxious. K.C. and Ashley showed us the courtroom. Ashley explained that we would be sitting in a place called the **witness stand**. She showed us the microphone where we'd speak. She showed us the chair where the judge sits. I asked her what the judge does. Ashley explained to us that the **judge presides over the trial**. It was his or her job to make sure that everything was fair and that everyone's **rights** were protected in the courtroom.

> **Rights:** in keeping with the rules of justice, law, or society.

> **Jury Box:** the usually enclosed place where the jury sits in a courtroom.
>
> **Jury:** a group of people called to a court of law who listen to the facts of a case and decide its outcome.
>
> **Alternate Jurors:** a juror who is selected in the same manner as a regular juror and hears the evidence in a case along with the regular jurors but does not help decide the case unless called upon to replace a regular juror.

Ashley and K.C. used a lot of big words that I didn't understand.

Ashley showed us the rows of seats called the **jury box**, where the **jury** sits. I asked what a Jury does. K.C. explained that the Jury is usually made up of 12 jurors, who are men and women who attend the trial, listen to the evidence and testimony given by witnesses. There are 12 jurors and usually two **alternate jurors**. She said at the end of the trial the jurors will **deliberate** and decide if there is enough evidence **to convict** or **acquit** the **accused party** called the **defendant**.

K.C. explained that our Poppy was the defendant.

The courtroom smelled moldy. The carpeting was old and stained. The wooden benches were shiny and had cushions.

The scariest part was when Ashley showed us where Poppy would be sitting. He was going to be sitting close to where Charlie and I would be sitting on the witness stand, too close, in my mind. I asked, "Will Poppy be able to hurt us?"

Ashley and K.C. both said he couldn't hurt us in the courtroom, but this didn't really make Charlie or me less scared about having to see Poppy.

> **Deliberate:** to think about an issue or question in a careful and thorough way, sometimes by discussing it with others.
>
> **To Convict:** to find guilty of a crime.
>
> **To Acquit:** to free from a charge of breaking the law; declare not guilty.
>
> **Accused Party:** a specific person who is blamed for or charged with a crime or with doing something wrong.
>
> **Defendant:** one who is accused or sued in a court of law.

"The scariest part was when Ashley showed us where Poppy would be sitting."

Ashley told us that some witnesses can get emotional support from a support dog, who sits with them during interviews with prosecutors, **defense attorneys**, or when they testify in court. Sadly, this didn't work out for our case because Charlie is allergic to dogs.

> **Defense Attorney:** the attorney representing the defendant in a lawsuit or criminal prosecution.

Every time we'd meet with K.C. and Ashley, K.C. would tell us that what happened to us was not our fault. K.C. was kind. She could tell we were scared, but she always tried to make us feel safe. She told us a lot of information. It was hard to understand everything she was talking about. But she said it in a nice way, and I always felt better after talking to her. This is what another DA in the office, District Attorney Handley, told Charlie and me:

1. "Tell the truth, even if you think your Mama or Poppy will get mad at you or if you think they will get in trouble.
2. Ask questions. If you don't understand something, ask for an explanation. You're allowed to ask questions because it's your life and something happened to you. You have the right to know and understand what's happening.
3. Speak up. If you're scared or have a worry, say so. No one can read your mind, so you have to say what you're feeling or if you need something to help you feel more secure.
4. Know that it's not your fault. You did nothing wrong and didn't deserve any bad thing that happened to you. It doesn't change who you are inside.
5. Don't be afraid. The bad person is the one who should be scared."

Mama told us it was getting closer to the **trial**. We were going to something called the **pretrial interview**. We had lots of questions about what to expect at the pretrial interview. Mama said what she always said. "I can't tell you what to say. All I can tell you is to be brave. Tell the truth. Tell what you remember. You will be okay."

K.C. explained to us that the defense attorney may ask hard questions that seem unkind. She said that he might use big words that you don't understand. He might try to twist your words and confuse you.

The day came for the pretrial interviews. Uncle Hank came with us to the prosecutor's office. We sat in the oversized chairs and waited in the lobby to be called. This was our first time meeting the defense attorney.

Mama sat us down before we left the house. She was very serious. She explained that Mr. Gallegos was the **public defender**. She said, "It's Mr. Gallegos' job to defend your Poppy. You don't have to like him, but you must show him respect. He's doing his job."

The pretrial interview took place in the conference room at the prosecutor's office. Mr. Gallegos was a quiet man with a serious look on his face. K.C. and Ashley were in the room with us. Thankfully, Poppy wasn't there. I asked if Mama could come in with me, but they said she had to wait outside with Uncle Hank.

I remembered what she told me: "Be Brave. Tell the truth. Tell what you remember. You'll be okay."

> **Trial:** the act of hearing a case in court to decide whether a person has broken a particular law.
>
> **Pre-Trial Interview:** pre-trial is the time after an individual has been arrested but before they have been convicted of a crime. During this time period, a pretrial services officer will gather information about the defendant through interviews and record checks.
>
> **Public Defender:** an attorney who, at public expense, defends persons accused of crimes who are themselves unable to pay.

It's hard to remember everything about the pretrial interview. There were lots of questions. K.C. and Mr. Gallegos talked back and forth. I felt overwhelmed. Charlie and I were both glad when it was over. After the pretrial interviews, we walked to the Plaza and had double scoops of ice cream.

Mama told us that after the pretrial interviews the prosecutor would decide if they were going to offer Poppy a **plea bargain**. A plea deal allows the accused to confess to the crime and avoid a trial, in exchange for a reduced **sentence**. If Poppy said no to the plea bargain it meant, we would have to

> **Plea Bargain:** in criminal procedure, a negotiation between the defendant and his attorney on one side and the prosecutor on the other, in which the defendant agrees to plead "guilty" or "no contest" to some crimes, in return for reduction of the severity of the charges, dismissal of some of the charges, the prosecutor's willingness to recommend a particular sentence or some other benefit to the defendant.
>
> **Sentence:** a punishment for a particular crime decided and declared in a court of law.

go to trial and testify in the courthouse.

Mama said it wasn't our job to worry about any of these big-people problems. Sometimes, I had a hard time sleeping.

Charlie always went to the nurse's office at school. He told the nurse that he had "stress-ess-ess" about his Poppy.

> **Grooming:** one tool common to those who sexually abuse kids is grooming: manipulative behaviors that the abuser uses to gain access to a potential victim, coerce them to agree to the abuse, and reduce the risk of being caught. While these tactics are used most often against younger kids, teens and vulnerable adults are also at risk.

Mama took us to see counselors. She said that it would help us to have someone else to talk to besides her.

While we were waiting for the trial, I kept seeing my counselor, Kathryn, every week. Sometimes we talked about the yucky things that Poppy did with us. When I went to counseling, I started to understand that some of what Poppy did as play was called **grooming** or sexual abuse.

I had trouble controlling my anger. Counselor Kathryn was kind, funny and helped me to understand my feelings. She taught me things like taking deep breaths, going for a walk, or drawing pictures of my feelings. I liked Kathryn.

Charlie saw a counselor named Don. He was an older man with glasses. Charlie said he was kind, caring and understanding, but he didn't say much more.

Later, both therapists were **subpoenaed** to testify at Poppy's trial. This meant the court was ordering them to appear at Poppy's trial as witnesses.

As the trial approached, I felt scared. I wondered what would happen if Poppy didn't go to prison. Would we go back to him? Would he be able to keep sexually abusing us? Mama did her best to answer our questions and calm our "what-if's."

About a week before the trial Charlie was crying. He cried a lot. He was scared about having to see Poppy in court. Mama asked him if there was anything that would help him feel safer. Mama explained that she couldn't be there in the courtroom because she might be called as a **witness**. Charlie asked if it would be possible for a policeman to come with him to the courtroom. Mama called K.C. and Ashley to ask if this would be possible. K.C. got permission from the judge, who said that a police officer could accompany Charlie and me, but he couldn't be in his uniform because it might **prejudice the jury**.

Mama called the police department and spoke to the policeman in charge. She explained the situation and asked if there was an officer who would be willing to show-up for this uncommon

> **Subpoena/ed:** in law, a formal written order summoning a witness to give testimony or requiring that specified evidence be submitted.
>
> **Witness:** a person who gives evidence in a court of law.
>
> **Prejudice the Jury:** to change the way that members of the jury feel about the court case.

request. The policeman understood Mama's request. He said that Sergeant Steven Martinez would meet us at the district attorney's office the morning of the trial.

The day of the trial finally arrived. It was two years, five months, and twenty days since Charlie's fifth birthday when I told on Poppy.

Uncle Hank, Grandma, our Pastor Harry, and many friends came to support us at the trial. We got to spend the night in the big and fancy hotel on the Plaza in downtown

Las Vegas. We wore our best clothes, and Mama insisted we both have our hair cut.

Sergeant Martinez met Charlie and me at the prosecutor's office. He walked with Ashley and me to the courthouse. I held Ashley's hand. I wished Mama was with me. We passed through the metal detectors, walked up the stairs. Sergeant Martinez opened the door for us.

The room was silent when I walked in. I took off my glasses as Ashley had suggested. I could see that there were a lot of people there to support us, but everything was blurry without my glasses. Ashley held my hand and walked me up to the witness stand.

Sergeant Martinez sat in the aisle right behind Poppy. I felt safe. I knew that if Poppy tried anything crazy Sergeant Martinez would protect me.

During the time I had to testify, I was allowed to hold a small stuffed animal on my lap. When Charlie testified, he had a small, good-luck charm tucked into his pocket.

I don't remember much about this day. It's hard to explain, but I felt like I was in a dream. I can hardly remember anything that happened in the courtroom.

I remember Mr. Gallegos, the public defender, asked me if my Mama had told me what to say. I replied: "Yes… She told me to tell the truth."

K.C. and Mr. Gallegos took turns asking me questions. I did what Ashley suggested. I just kept looking at K.C.

Our pastor, Harry Eberts, came to the trial to support us. He described watching us testify:

"The heaviness of the proceedings seemed to be pressing down upon the room as we watched from the courtroom gallery. Most of us were… dressed up as if we were attending something **solemn** and **sacred**, which of course we were.

Solemn: serious in appearance, sound, or mood.
Sacred: solemn, spiritual.

It was solemn because of why we were there. It was unspeakable on most every other day, but Charlie and May spoke up on this day. They were **poised**. They were small. They smiled nervously at times. Yet they were larger than life, rising above what had happened to them, bringing it out in the open for all to hear, instead of keeping the fear

> **Shame:** to cause loss of respect; bring embarrassment to.
>
> **Strength:** the state, quality, or condition of being strong.
>
> **Protest:** an expression of being against something; objection; complaint.

and **shame** inside and shut away. Then they answered questions about what their father did to them.

Charlie, I remember thinking, seemed so tall as he spoke, and that came not from height but from an inner **strength** that he holds. I have no idea how he did it. May, too, perhaps even more so because of her age.

I don't remember what each of them said. Showing up was enough. Giving short answers to difficult questions was enough. Sitting in the same room with their dad was more than enough, more than brave. Not sure there is a word for it…

Healing happens when the light of day shines on terrible things and voices rise in **protest**, or for these two **brave** children, when they lead to a reckoning and a new beginning.

It was sacred because all of life is sacred, even in the worst of times and the bravest of times, and even in those times

"My mother told me to tell the truth."

Brave: ready to face pain or danger, courageous.

> **Abusive:** characterized by injurious or offensive treatment.
>
> **Sentencing Hearing:** the court process where the judge decides the defendant's penalty.

when life can't get any harder. I imagined that giving testimony against an **abusive** parent would be one of the hardest things anyone would ever be asked to do. And Charlie and May did it. They survived and they will always know they did."

The jury deliberated and issued a verdict. Poppy was found guilty of sexual abuse.

The day Poppy was convicted, I felt relieved, but Mama told us that we couldn't relax until he was sentenced.

The next morning, Mama, Uncle Hank, and Granny got dressed up. I barely recognized Uncle Hank not wearing his flip flops, shorts, and a t-shirt. Our favorite babysitter, Lydia, came to Granny's house to stay with us while the family went to Las Vegas for the sentencing hearing.

Mama hugged us both tightly. She said she loved us. She told us that no matter how the **sentencing hearing** went, she was proud of us for being brave.

When Mama came home, she looked happy and relaxed. I don't remember the last time I saw her smile.

Mama sat down with us on Granny's couch. I could see she was holding back tears. She explained that the judge had sentenced Poppy to 36 years in prison.

Charlie asked Mama if it was still okay for him to pray for Poppy. She said it was okay.

I'm a little sad that I didn't get a chance to say goodbye to my Poppy, but I'm glad he's in prison. I feel safe knowing that Poppy can't hurt Charlie and me or any other kids.

After the trial, K.C. told us that finding **closure** is a long road. She said now that justice was served, we could begin our journey to becoming survivors.

If you were sexually abused, you might have to testify at a trial, just like us. I know you can do it.

Just be brave. Tell the truth. Tell what you remember. You'll be okay.

Closure: an ending or concluding.

Glossary of Terms

Safe Adult: someone a child can go to if they ever feel unsafe, have been hurt, or if they're not sure if a situation is unsafe.

Sexual Abuse: When a perpetrator intentionally harms a minor physically, psychologically, sexually, or by acts of neglect, the crime is known as child abuse.

Sexual Assault Nurse Examiner (SANE): a registered nurse who completed additional education and training to provide comprehensive health care to survivors of sexual assault.

Evidence: something that gives proof or reason to believe.

Trial: the act of hearing a case in court to decide whether a person has broken a particular law.

Testify: to make a solemn declaration or affirmation, esp. under oath.

Social Worker: a worker who promotes the well-being of society, as by assisting the underprivileged or disadvantaged.

Child Protective Services: a branch of your state's social services department that is responsible for the assessment, investigation, and intervention regarding cases of child abuse and neglect, including sexual abuse.

Investigating the crime: a careful and close look into something that is against the law to learn the facts.

Forensic Interview/er: A forensic interview is a non-leading, developmentally sensitive method of gathering information from children. These recorded statements are conducted by a specially trained, unbiased professional in a legally defensible manner.

Prosecutor: an attorney who prosecutes, esp. when serving as an official of a county, district, or other government entity.

District Attorney: an elected official of a county or a designated district with the responsibility for prosecuting crimes.

Deputy District Attorney: an assistant who works under the supervision of a district attorney in carrying out prosecution duties for both misdemeanor and felony court cases.

Victim Advocate: a person, whether paid or serving as a volunteer, who provides services to victims of domestic violence, sexual assault, stalking, or dating violence under the auspices or supervision of a victim services program.

Victim/s: someone who is hurt, injured, or killed by a person, group, or event.

Perpetrate/d: to commit or carry out (a crime, act of mischief, or the like).

Survivor: a person who continues to function or prosper despite a situation.

Traumatic: an emotional shock that has a deep effect on one's life for a long time.

Resiliency: the capacity to withstand and recover quickly from difficulty, sickness, or the like.

Justice: the upholding of what is just, fair, and right.

Courthouse: a building where courts of law and other government offices are located.

Court: a place where legal cases are heard.

Metal detectors: a device that detects and signals the presence of metal objects and is used to discover concealed weapons at a security point.

Witness stand: the place in a court of law from which a witness testifies.

Judge: a person trained to hear and decide cases brought before a court of law.

Preside (over a) Trial: to act as the one in charge of the act of hearing a case in court to decide whether a person has broken a particular law.

Trial: the act of hearing a case in court to decide whether a person has broken a particular law.

Rights: in keeping with the rules of justice, law, or society.

Jury Box: the usually enclosed place where the jury sits in a courtroom.

Jury: a group of people called to a court of law who listen to the facts of a case and decide its outcome.

Alternate Jurors: a juror who is selected in the same manner as a regular juror and hears the evidence in a case along with the regular jurors but does not help decide the case unless called upon to replace a regular juror.

Deliberate: to think about an issue or question in a careful and thorough way, sometimes by discussing them with others.

To Convict: to find guilty of a crime.

To Acquit: to free from a charge of breaking the law; declare not guilty.

Accused Party: a specific person who is blamed for or charged with a crime or with doing something wrong.

Defendant: one who is accused or sued in a court of law.

Pre-Trial Interview: Pre-trial is the time period after an individual has been arrested but before they have been convicted of a crime. During this time period, a pretrial services officer will gather information about the defendant through interviews and record checks.

Defense Attorney: the attorney representing the defendant in a lawsuit or criminal prosecution.

Public Defender: an attorney who, at public expense, defends persons accused of crimes who are themselves unable to pay.

Plea Bargain: in criminal procedure, a negotiation between the defendant and his attorney on one side and the prosecutor on the other, in which the defendant agrees to plead "guilty" or "no contest" to some crimes, in return for reduction of the severity of the charges, dismissal of some of the charges, the prosecutor's willingness to recommend a particular sentence or some other benefit to the defendant.

Witness: a person who gives evidence in a court of law.

Prejudice the Jury: to change the way that members of the jury feel about the court case.

Solemn: serious in appearance, sound, or mood.

Sacred: solemn, spiritual.

Poised: the ability to act in a calm and confident manner.

Shame: to cause loss of respect; bring embarrassment to.

Strength: the state, quality, or condition of being strong.

Protest: an expression of being against something; objection; complaint.

Brave: ready to face pain or danger, courageous.

Reckoning: to expect or judge that.

Abusive: characterized by injurious or offensive treatment.

Verdict: the decision of a judge or jury in a law case.

To Find Guilty: a court determination that one has been found responsible for breaking a law or doing something wrong.

Grooming: One tool common to those who sexually abuse kids is grooming: manipulative behaviors that the abuser uses to gain access to a potential victim, coerce them to agree to the abuse, and reduce the risk of being caught. While these tactics are used most often against younger kids, teens and vulnerable adults are also at risk.

Sentence: a punishment for a particular crime decided and declared in a court of law.

Sentencing Hearing: the court process where the judge decides the defendant's penalty.

Subpoena: in law, a formal written order summoning a witness to give testimony or requiring that specified evidence be submitted.
Prison: a building for holding and punishing people who have broken the law.
Closure: an ending or concluding.

Acknowledgements and Special Thanks

My family
Hector Balderas Attorney General, New Mexico (2015-2022)
Teresa Casados
Dave Yount
Tracy Leonard, Subject matter expert advisor
Kelly Jensen, Editor
Sonja Fleming, Literary Consultant
Bryan McKay
K.C. Carmona
Brittany Du Chaussee
Collin Brennan
Zachary Jones
Richard O'Leary
Victoria Bransford
Jerri Mares
Brian Colon,
August E. Perez, MA, LPC
David J. Romero Sr., MA, LPCC
Don Chavez
Kathryn Rice
Julie Wittenberger
Deborah Cornelius (In Memoriam)
Linda Lapcik
Aleida van Aken
Rika Meade (and the B's)
Thomas Clayton District Attorney, 4th Judicial District, New Mexico
Jane Handley
Jason Kramer, Attorney, Subject Matter Consultant
Cynthia Cushman
Julia Ressl
Jeff Oliver
Nancy Dahl
Kit Ayala
Holly Kinley
Jacqueline Rea
Kimberly King, Literary Consultant, Author: Kimberly King Books
Barbara Romo, District Attorney, 13th Judicial District, literary contributor: Foreword
Joline Gutierrez-Krueger, Columnist
Richard Eeds, Radio Show Host
Lorene Mills, TV Journalist
Troy Baker
Rollin Tyler Jones, Fire Fighter
Bruce and Mary Black

Ashley Archuleta, Victim Advocate
Lauren Dachman, Trauma Counselor
Cleo Gonzales, Las Vegas District Attorney's Office
Clay Goret, New Mexico State Police
Steven Martinez, New Mexico State Police
Jerry Santana, New Mexico State Police
Wilson Silver, New Mexico State Police
Pastor Harry Eberts III, Pastor, First Presbyterian Church of Santa Fe
Richard and Laura Bank
Daniela Kestleman
Chico Gallegos, Defense Attorney
Anne Marie Lynch
Cliff Rees
Jefferson Davis, M.D.
Matt Baca
Lizzie Aragon
Katheryn Wallace
Lydia Cort
Susan Cort
Wendy Gordon (In Memoriam)
Cecilia Conley (In Memoriam)
Lisa Weisenfeld, Attorney
Sheila Lewis, Attorney
Amanda Kennemore
Miranda Viscoli, Co-President of New Mexicans to Prevent Gun Violence

Anna Llobet-Megias
Connie Warren, Victim Advocate
Khia Khan
Bobbie Ingersoll, Literary Consultant
Tracy Orwig, Assistant Professor of Social Work, University of Texas
Arthrell Family
Maureen Drexell
Yvonne Villescas
Karleen Gonzales
Paulette Miller
Raul Esparza
Jennifer Conn
Ane Romero
Pamela Garcia
Roberta Colton
Michael Knuckey
Elaine McCarthy
Sandra Dransfield
Brandon Burelle
Jackie Ewer
Kayla Sharpe
Cindy Weaver
Deanna Heimsoth
Anne Liliey
Jill McCormick
John Delamater
Paul Joye
Shari Watson

Bibliography

"Abusive." Kids.Wordsmyth, https://www.kids.wordsmyth.net/we/?ent=abusive.

Accused Party:

"Accused." KidsWordsmyth, https://www.kidswordsmyth.net/we/accused.

"Party." KidsWordsmyth, https://www.kidswordsmyth.net/we/?ent=party.

"Alternate Jurors." FindLaw, https://www.dictionary.findlaw.com/definition/alternate-juror.html.

"Brave." Kids.Wordsmyth, https://www.kidswordsmyth.net/we/?ent=brave.

"Child Protective Services." StopItNow!, https://www.stopitnow.org/ohc-content/what-is-child-protective-services.

"Closure." KidsWordsmyth, https://www.kids.wordsmyth.net/we/?ent=closure.

"Convict." KidsWordsmyth, https://www.kids.wordsmyth.net/we?ent=convict.

"Courthouse." KidsWordsmyth, https://www.kids.wordsmyth.net/we?ent=courthouse.

"Court." KidsWordsmyth, https://kids.wordsmyth.net/we/?ent=court

"Defense Attorney." Law.com: Services & Resources Legal Dictionary, https://www.dictionary.law.com/Default.aspx?typed=defense%20attorney&type=1.

"Defendant." KidsWordsmyth, https://www.kidswordsmyth.net/we?ent=defendant.

"To Convict." KidsWordsmyth, https://kids.wordsmyth.net/we/?ent=to+convict

"Subpoena." KidsWordsmyth, https://kids.wordsmyth.net/we/?ent=subpoena

"Deliberate." KidsWordsmyth, https://www.kidswordsmyth.net/we?ent=deliberate.

"Deputy District Attorney." Practical Adult Insights, https://www.practicaladultinsights.com/what-does-a-deputy-district-attorney-do.htm.

"District Attorney." Law.com: Services & Resources Legal Dictionary, https://www.dictionary.law.com/Default.aspx?typed=district%20attorney&type=1.

Eberts III, Harry. Personal Interview. 05 Feb. 2022.

"Evidence." KidsWordsmyth, https://www.kids.wordsmyth.net/we?ent=evidence.

Forensic Interview/er: https://centerforchildprotection.org/services/forensic-services/

"Grooming." RAINN, https://www.rainn.org/news/grooming-know-warning-signs

"Forensic." KidsWordsmyth, https://www.kidswordsmyth.net/we?ent=forensic.

Handley, Jane. Personal Interview. 19 Jan. 2022.

Investigating the Crime:

"Investigate." KidsWordsmyth, https://www.kidswordsmyth.net/we?ent=investigate.

"Crime." KidsWordsmyth, https://www.kidswordsmyth.net/we?ent=crime.

"Judge." KidsWordsmyth, https://www.kidswordsmyth.net/we?ent=judge.

"Jury." KidsWordsmyth, https://www.kidswordsmyth.net/we?ent=jury.

"Jury Box." Merriam-Webster Dictionary, https://www.merriam-webster.com/legal/jury%20box.

"Justice." KidsWordsmyth, https://www.kidswordsmyth.net/we?ent=justice.

"Metal Detectors." KidsWordsmyth, https://www.kidswordsmyth.net/we?ent=metaldetector.

"Perpetrate/d." KidsWordsmyth, https://www.kidswordsmyth.net/we?ent=perpetrate.

"Plea Bargain." Law.com: Services & Resources, https://www.dictionary.law.com/Defaultaspx?typed=plea%20bargain&type=1.

"Poised." KidsWordsmyth, https://www.kidswordsmyth.net/we?ent=poised.

Prejudice the Jury:

"Prejudice." KidsWordsmyth, https://www.kidswordsmyth.net/we?ent=prejudice.

"Jury." KidsWordsmyth, https://www.kidswordsmyth.net/we?ent=jury.

Preside over a Trial:

"Preside." KidsWordsmyth, https://www.kidswordsmyth.net/we?ent=preside.

"Trial." KidsWordsmyth, https://www.kidswordsmyth.net/we?ent=trial.

"Pre-trial Interview." Google, google.com/search?q=pretrial+interview+definintion&rlz=1CAMFAZ_enUS970US970

"Prosecutor." KidsWordsmyth, https://www.kidswordsmyth.net/we?ent=prosecutor.

"Protest." KidsWordsmyth, https://www.kidswordsmyth.net/we?ent=protest.

"Reckoning." KidsWordsmyth, https://www.kidswordsmyth.net/we?ent=reckoning.

"Resiliency." KidsWordsmyth, https://www.kidswordsmyth.net/we?ent=resiliency.

"Rights." KidsWordsmyth, https://www.kidswordsmyth.net/we?ent=rights.

"Sacred." KidsWordsmyth, https://www.kidswordsmyth.net/we?ent=sacred.

"Safe Adult." Monique Burr: Foundation for Children Prevention Education Programs, https://www.mbfpreventioneducation.org/safe-adults/.

"Sentence." KidsWordsmyth, https://www.kidswordsmyth.net/we?ent=sentence.

"Sentence Hearing." Google, https://www.google.com/search?q=sentencing+hearing+definition&rlz=1CAMFAZ_enU

"Sexual Abuse." RAINN, https://www.rainn.org/articles/child-sexual-abuse

"Sexual Assault Nurse Examiner (SANE)." Office of Justice Programs: Office for Victims of Crime, https://www.ovcttac.gov/saneguide/introduction/what-is-a-sane/.

"Shame." KidsWordsmyth, https://www.kidswordsmyth.net/we?ent=shame.

"Social Worker." KidsWordsmyth, https://www.kidswordsmyth.net/we?ent=social+worker.

"Solemn." KidsWordsmyth, https://www.kidswordsmyth.net/we?ent=solemn.

"Strength." KidsWordsmyth, https://www.kidswordsmyth.net/we?ent=strength.

"Survivor." Merriam-Webster Dictionary, https://www.merriam-webster.com/dictionary/survivor.

"To Find Guilty." KidsWordsmyth, https://www.kidswordsmyth.net/we?ent=guilty.

"Testify." KidsWordsmyth, https://www.kidswordsmyth.net/we?ent=testify.

"Traumatic." KidsWordsmyth, https://www.kidswordsmyth.net/we?ent=traumatic.

"Trial." KidsWordsmyth, https://www.kidswordsmyth.net/we?ent=trial.

"Verdict." KidsWordsmyth, https://www.kidswordsmyth.net/we?ent=verdict.

"Victim." KidsWordsmyth, https://www.kidswordsmyth.net/we?ent=victim.

"Victim's Advocate." Cornell Law, https://www.law.cornell.edu/definitions/uscode.php?width=840&height=800&iframe=true&def_id=34-USC-1003300355-1259336258&term_occur=999&term_src=.

"Witness." KidsWordsmyth, https://www.kidswordsmyth.net/we?ent=witness.

"Witness Stand." https://kids.wordsmyth.net/we/?ent=Witness+stand

www.ingramcontent.com/pod-product-compliance
Lightning Source LLC
Chambersburg PA
CBHW042354070526
44585CB00028B/2924